VOYAGE OF A LIGHT BEAM

Andrew Solway

www.raintreepublishers.co.uk
Visit our website to find out more information about **Raintree** books.

To order:

 Phone 44 (0) 1865 888112

 Send a fax to 44 (0) 1865 314091

 Visit the Raintree bookshop at **www.raintreepublishers.co.uk** to browse our catalogue and order online.

First published in Great Britain by Raintree, Halley Court, Jordan Hill, Oxford OX2 8EJ, part of Harcourt Education.
Raintree is a registered trademark of Harcourt Education Ltd.

Editorial: Lucy Thunder and Richard Woodham
Design: Victoria Bevan and Kamae Design
Illustrations: Kamae Design
Picture Research: Melissa Allison and Kay Altwegg
Production: Camilla Crask

Originated by Dot Gradations Ltd
Printed and bound in Italy by Printer Trento srl

ISBN 1 844 43855 4 (hardback)
10 09 08 07 06
10 9 8 7 6 5 4 3 2 1

ISBN 1 844 43970 4 (paperback)
11 10 09 08 07
10 9 8 7 6 5 4 3 2 1

British Library Cataloguing in Publication Data
Solway, Andrew
Voyage of a Light Beam: Light
535
A full catalogue record for this book is available from the British Library.

Acknowledgements
The publishers would like to thank the following for permission to reproduce photographs:
Corbis p. 6–7; Galaxy Picture Library pp. 8–9, 16–17, 26–27; Science Photo Library pp. 4–5 (NASA), 10–11 (NASA), 14–15 (Detlev Van Ravenswaay), 18–19 (Planetary Visions Ltd), 20–21.

Cover photograph of Earth and Sun, reproduced with permission of Science Photo Library/NIBSC.

The publishers would like to thank Nancy Harris and Harold Pratt for their assistance in the preparation of this book.

Every effort has been made to contact copyright holders of any material reproduced in this book. Any omissions will be rectified in subsequent printings if notice is given to the publishers.

The paper used to print this book comes from sustainable resources.

Disclaimer
All the Internet addresses (URLs) given in this book were valid at the time of going to press. However, due to the dynamic nature of the Internet, some addresses may have changed, or sites may have changed or ceased to exist since publication. While the author and publishers regret any inconvenience this may cause readers, no responsibility for any such changes can be accepted by either the author or the publishers.

Contents

Some words are printed in bold, **like this**. You can find out what they mean on page 30. You can also look in the box at the bottom of the page where they first appear.

A high-speed trip

You are going on the trip of a lifetime! It's a trip across part of our **galaxy**. You will see many **stars**. You will also see Earth.

Have you ever thought about the stars you can see in the night sky? Each one is a huge ball of gas like our Sun. They look so tiny in the sky because they are very far away.

We are going to take a trip from one of those stars to Earth. The trip would take thousands of years in a spacecraft. We need something a bit quicker. We are going to follow a beam of light.

Light is a kind of **energy**. Light is like all energy. It can make things change. Light allows us to see things. We'll find out how on our trip.

energy	ability to make things move or change
galaxy	enormous group of stars
star	huge burning ball of gas

▼ This is the Apollo 10. *It is one of the fastest spacecraft. Even in this spacecraft our trip would take thousands of years. Light can travel a lot faster.*

You probably already know ▼ some things about light. Light always travels in a straight line unless something makes it change direction.

6

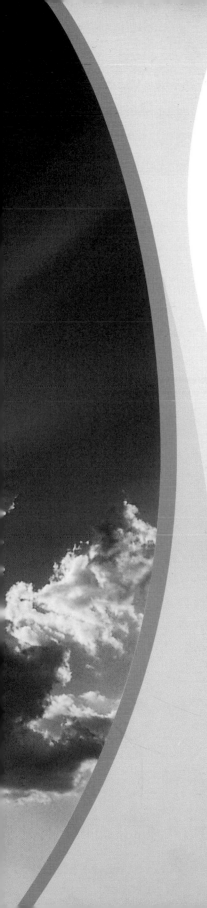

The fastest thing there is

Why follow a beam of light? Because it is the fastest thing there is. When we switch on a lamp the light is just there. It is all over the room, all at once. But light does not really reach everywhere all at once. It travels at a speed of about 300,000 kilometres (186,000 miles) each second!

At the speed of light you could get to the Moon in just over a second. You could reach the Sun in about 8 minutes. So fasten your seat belt!

Light fantastic:

* *light is a kind of **energy***
* *most of the light we get on Earth is from the Sun*
* *some other light sources include light bulbs, candles, fires, or other **stars***
* *light beams travel in straight lines*

A star in the Swan

Our light beam is starting from a **star** called Deneb. From Earth, Deneb looks like a tiny point of light. In fact, it is 60 times bigger than the Sun. It shines 60,000 times more brightly. But it is more than 100,000,000 times further away!

Deneb looks so small because it is so far away. It is 15,200,000,000,000,000 kilometres (9,400,000,000,000,000 miles) from Earth. This makes it one of the furthest stars we can see. A light beam is the fastest thing there is. But it still takes many years to travel from Deneb to Earth. So we had better get going!

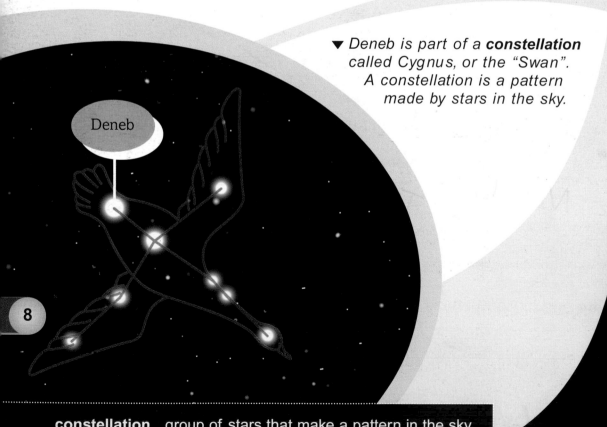

▼ *Deneb is part of a **constellation** called Cygnus, or the "Swan". A constellation is a pattern made by stars in the sky.*

Deneb

constellation   group of stars that make a pattern in the sky
light year   distance light travels in a year – 9500 billion kilometres (5900 billion miles)

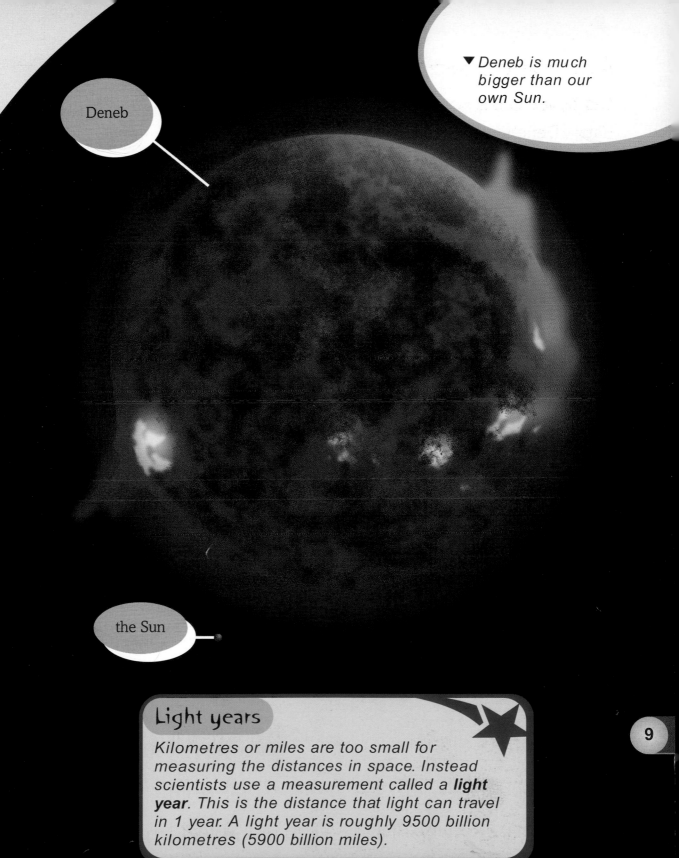

Deneb

▼ Deneb is much bigger than our own Sun.

the Sun

Light years

Kilometres or miles are too small for measuring the distances in space. Instead scientists use a measurement called a **light year**. This is the distance that light can travel in 1 year. A light year is roughly 9500 billion kilometres (5900 billion miles).

Light beam from Deneb

The **star** Deneb is a huge ball of gas. It is hotter than any fire on Earth. A star creates huge amounts of **energy**. A lot of this energy is heat and light.

Deneb is always giving out light. The light shines out in all directions. We are going to follow a light beam all the way to Earth. It must be going in exactly the right direction. This is important because you can't steer a light beam. It only goes straight ahead!

OK, so we know the direction to Earth. Now we pick a light beam, and off we go!

This photo shows that ▶ the Sun is a swirling ball of gas, just like Deneb. It creates light energy, too.

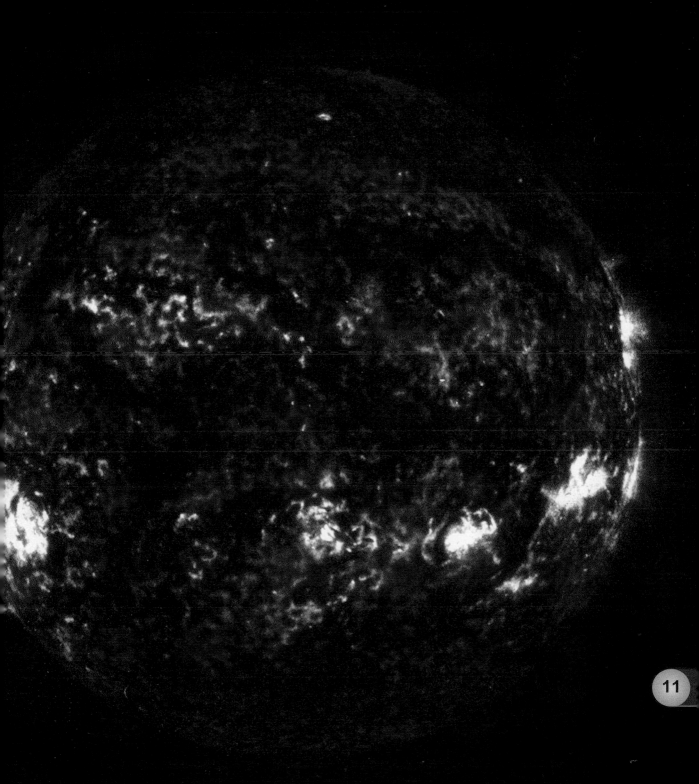

Where are we going?

Earth is part of a **galaxy** called the Milky Way. The galaxy is very large. We are travelling 1600 light years from Deneb to Earth. But we will cross only a small part of this galaxy.

The Milky Way has a bright centre called the hub. The hub is packed with billions of **stars**. Spiral arms spread out from the hub. Our Sun is near one of these arms. It is called the Orion arm. Deneb is near the Orion arm, too.

At the start of the journey we travel through empty space. There is nothing to see. Then a big ball of rock appears ahead. It's a planet. It looks like we are heading straight for it!

Speedy Scientist

Albert Einstein was a famous scientist. He lived from 1879 to 1955. He started thinking about the speed of light when he was just 16 years old. Later he worked out that nothing could travel faster than the speed of light.

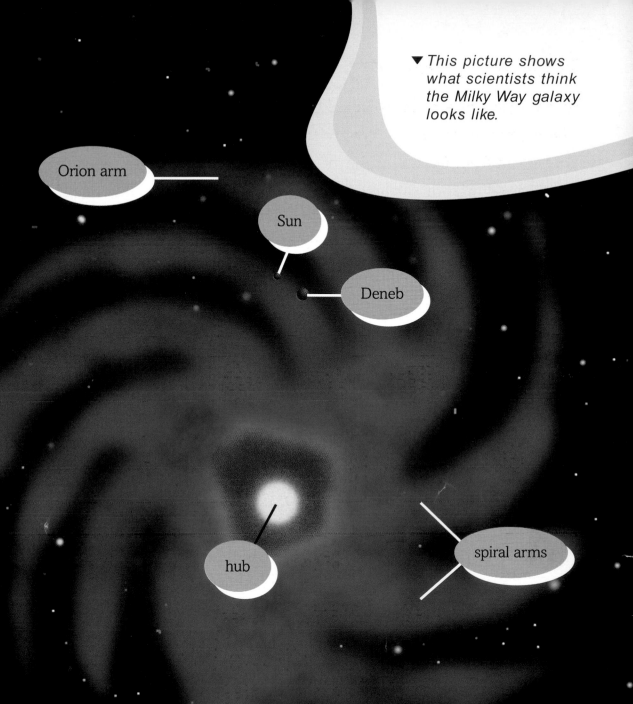

▼ *This picture shows what scientists think the Milky Way galaxy looks like.*

Planets and nebulas

Most of the time, light can travel through space without any problem. Much of space is **transparent**. There is nothing to stop light getting through. A planet is different. It is **opaque**. This means it does not let light through.

We won't make it to Earth if our light beam hits this planet! You can't steer a light beam. We can only wait and see what happens. Luckily our light beam misses the planet and shoots straight on.

Many other light beams from Deneb head straight into the planet. Some of them are taken in by the rocks. They are **absorbed**. Others are **reflected**. They bounce off in all directions.

Warming light

*Remember that light is a kind of **energy**? The light beams that are absorbed by the rocks don't just disappear. They make something happen. The light energy warms up the rocks.*

absorbed	taken in	**reflected**	bounced off
opaque	something that stops light passing through it	**transparent**	something that lets light pass through it

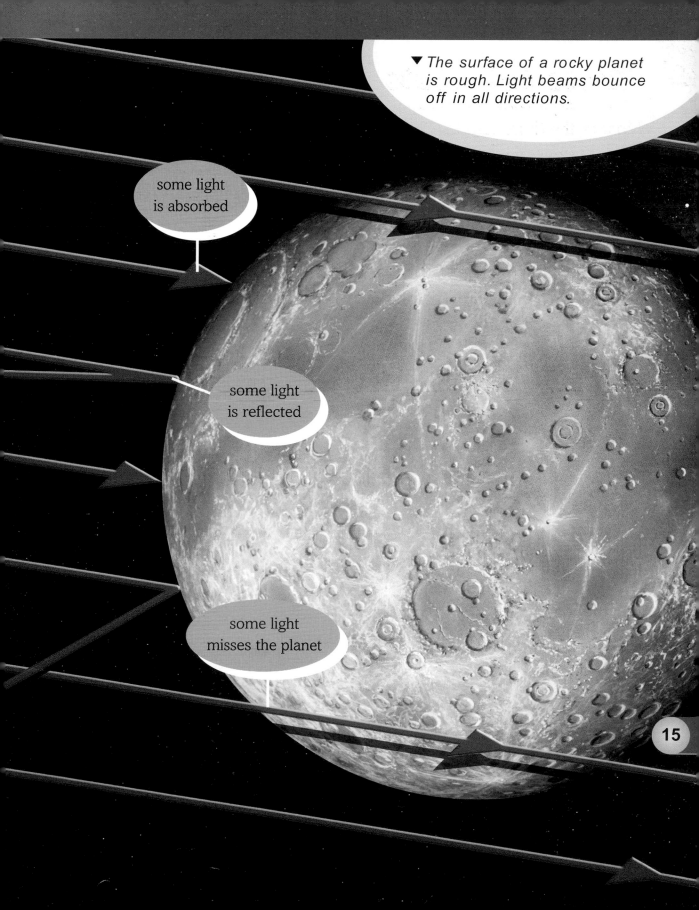

Shining gas clouds

We are out into deep space now. There is nothing for millions of kilometres. Far in the distance there is a fuzzy-looking light. As we get closer we see that it is an enormous cloud of gas and dust. It is a **nebula**. Parts of the nebula are glowing brightly.

This time, our light beam does not miss. It goes straight into the nebula. Will it get through? Some light beams are taken in. They are **absorbed** by the gas and dust in the nebula. The light **energy** makes the gas glow. Luckily, our light beam gets through. It has not changed.

Nebulas

Nebulas are huge clouds of gas and dust. Different things can make a nebula. Some nebulas are left over from giant stars that have exploded. Others are "star nurseries", where new stars are being made.

nebula   enormous cloud of gas and dust in space

In Earth's shadow

We've been following the light beam for almost 1600 years now. We're only minutes from the end of our journey. We've been travelling through empty space ever since we left the **nebula**. At least time flies when you're having fun!

When we left Deneb our light beam was part of an enormous blaze of light. But some of the light beams were **absorbed**, or taken in, by the nebula. Others **reflected** (bounced) off objects in space. Now only a few beams of light from Deneb are left.

A white **star** appears ahead. It's the Sun! Soon you can see Earth, too. It is between you and the Sun. It's approaching fast! The side of Earth facing you is in **shadow**. It is dark.

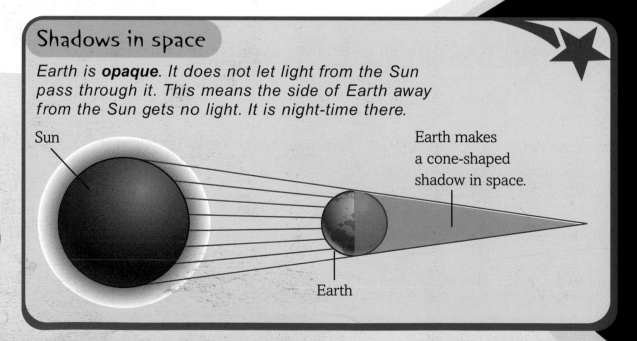

Shadows in space

*Earth is **opaque**. It does not let light from the Sun pass through it. This means the side of Earth away from the Sun gets no light. It is night-time there.*

Sun

Earth makes a cone-shaped shadow in space.

Earth

shadow   patch of darkness made when an object is blocking out light

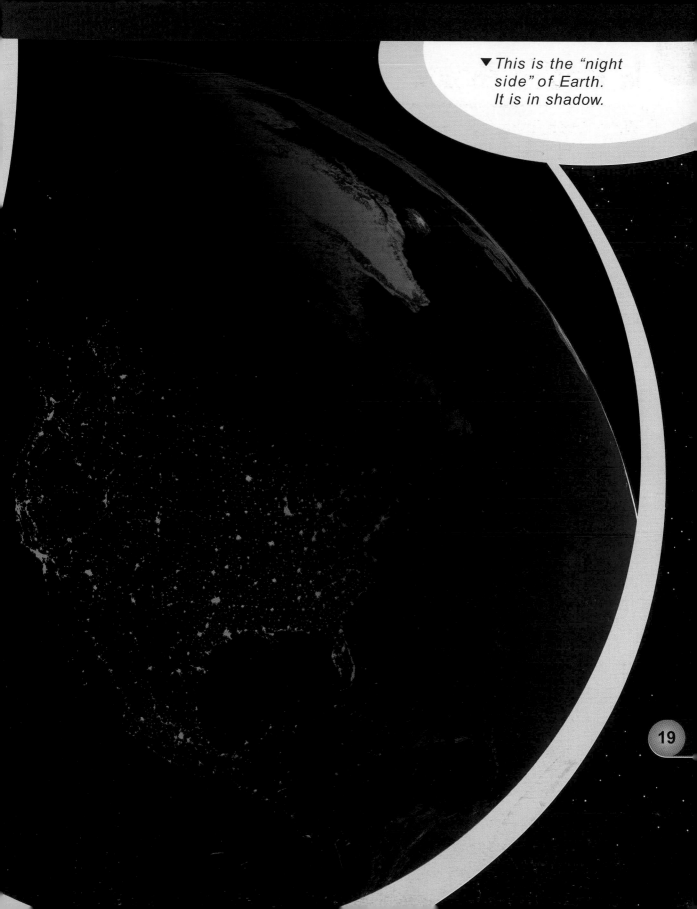

▼ *This is the "night side" of Earth. It is in shadow.*

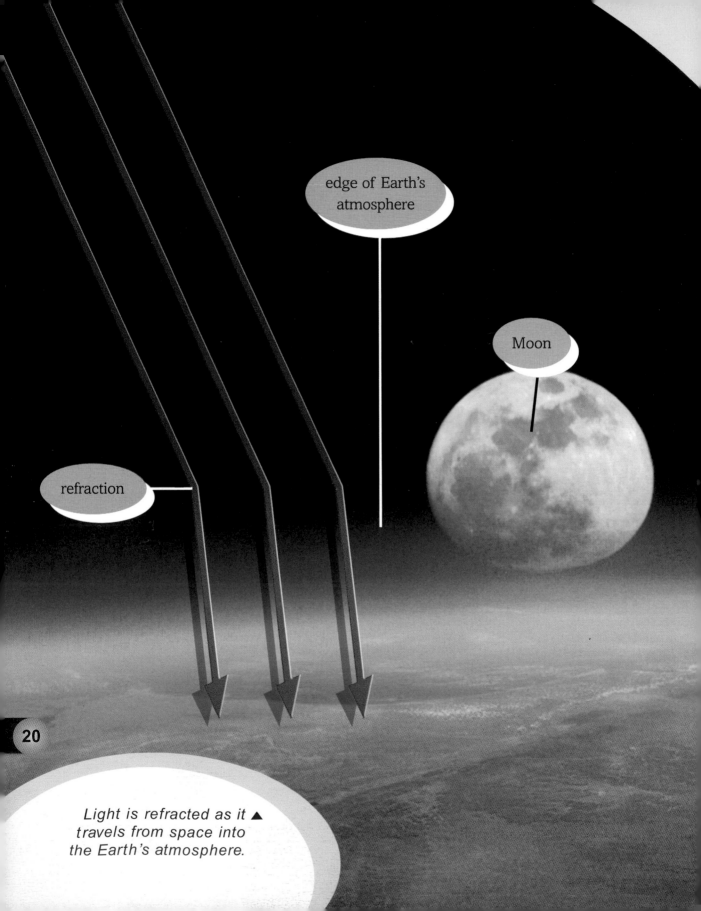

edge of Earth's atmosphere

Moon

refraction

20

Light is refracted as it ▲ travels from space into the Earth's atmosphere.

Approaching Earth

A lot of things happen in the next few seconds. First, our light beam just misses the Moon. A second later, our beam reaches a layer of air around the Earth. This is the Earth's **atmosphere**.

The light beam has travelled in a straight line for 1600 years. But now it is changing direction! Why? The light beam went in a straight line because it was travelling through space. Space is a **transparent** material. A transparent material lets light pass through it. The Earth's atmosphere is a different transparent material. When light hits the atmosphere it bends. When light moves from one transparent material to another the change can make the light bend. This is called **refraction**.

atmosphere   layer of air around Earth
refraction   way that light bends when it moves from one transparent material to another

Bouncing and bending

Our light beam zooms through Earth's **atmosphere** to the ground. There are still some other light beams from Deneb with it. More light beams are following behind. Some of them hit the ground and are **absorbed**. Some bounce off in different directions. But our light beam goes down a large tube. At the bottom is a curved, shiny mirror. We are inside a telescope!

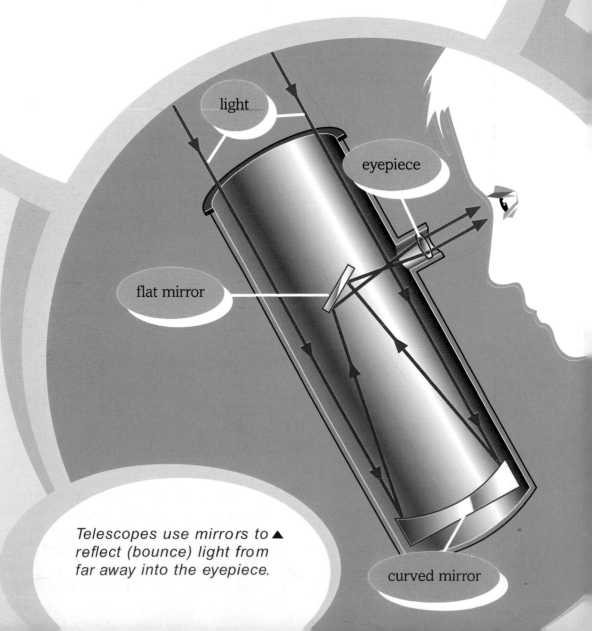

light

eyepiece

flat mirror

curved mirror

Telescopes use mirrors to ▲ reflect (bounce) light from far away into the eyepiece.

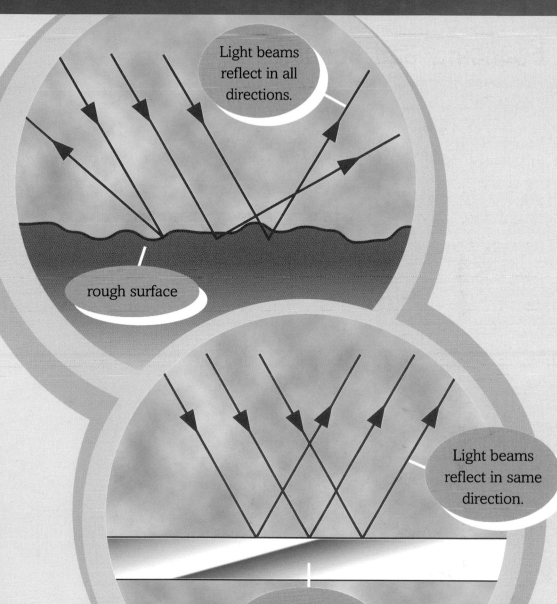

Light beams reflect in all directions.

rough surface

Light beams reflect in same direction.

smooth surface of mirror

Reflecting off mirrors

Light **reflects**, or bounces off, in all directions when it hits most surfaces. This is because most surfaces are rough to a light beam even if they feel smooth to us. A mirror is different. It is so smooth that light beams hitting it from one direction all bounce off again in the same direction.

A twinkle in the eye

Our light beam is almost at the end of its trip. It comes out of the telescope. Then it shoots into someone's eye. Other light beams from Deneb have made it this far. They shoot into the person's eye, too.

As they move from the air into the eye, the light beams are **refracted**. They are bent. The light beams are refracted again as they pass through the **lens** of the eye. All the beams are **focused** by the lens on to one spot at the back of the eye. The back of the eye is called the **retina**. The beams make a tiny image of Deneb on the retina.

focus   bring light beams together to make a clear picture
lens   curved piece of glass or other material
retina   coating on the back of the eye that picks up light

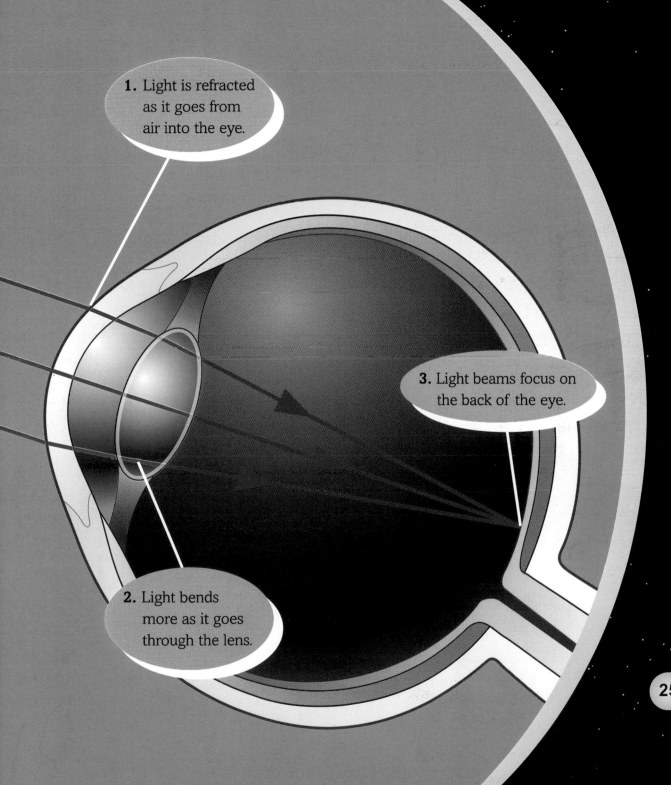

25

The journey ends

This is where our light beam ends its journey. At the back of the eye is the **retina**. This is the part of the eye that picks up light. The retina **absorbs** our light beam. But remember that light is **energy**. Energy can make things happen. What happens is that a picture of a tiny star is sent through **nerves** to the brain. The person sees Deneb!

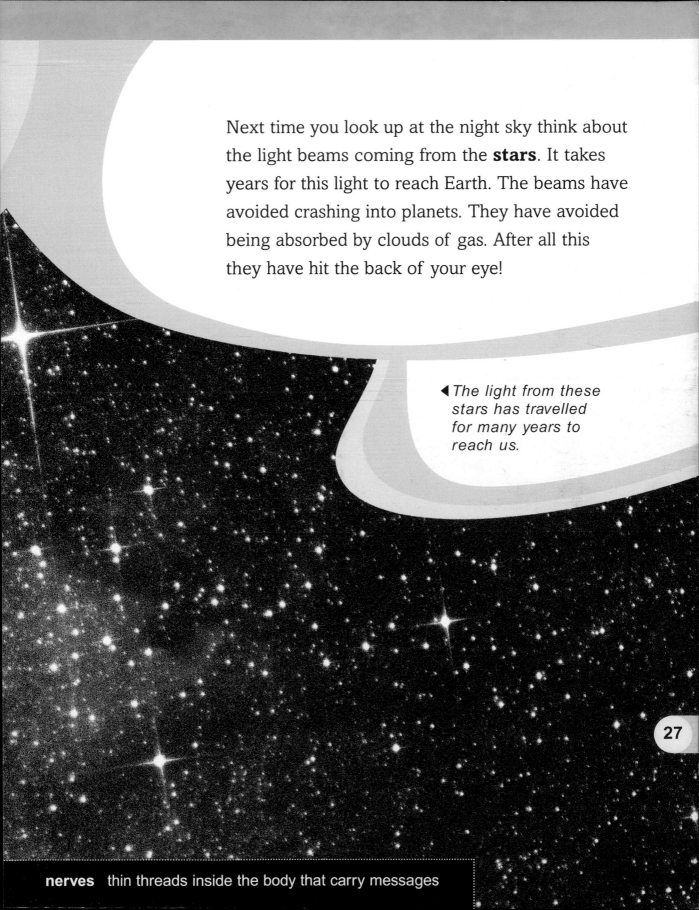

Next time you look up at the night sky think about the light beams coming from the **stars**. It takes years for this light to reach Earth. The beams have avoided crashing into planets. They have avoided being absorbed by clouds of gas. After all this they have hit the back of your eye!

◄ *The light from these stars has travelled for many years to reach us.*

nerves thin threads inside the body that carry messages

Voyage from a star

These are just some of the things that might happen to a light beam on a journey from a **star**.

The light beam bounces off the rough surface of a planet. It is **reflected**.

The light beam sets off on its journey. It travels in a straight line unless something affects it.

The light beam starts its journey from this star.

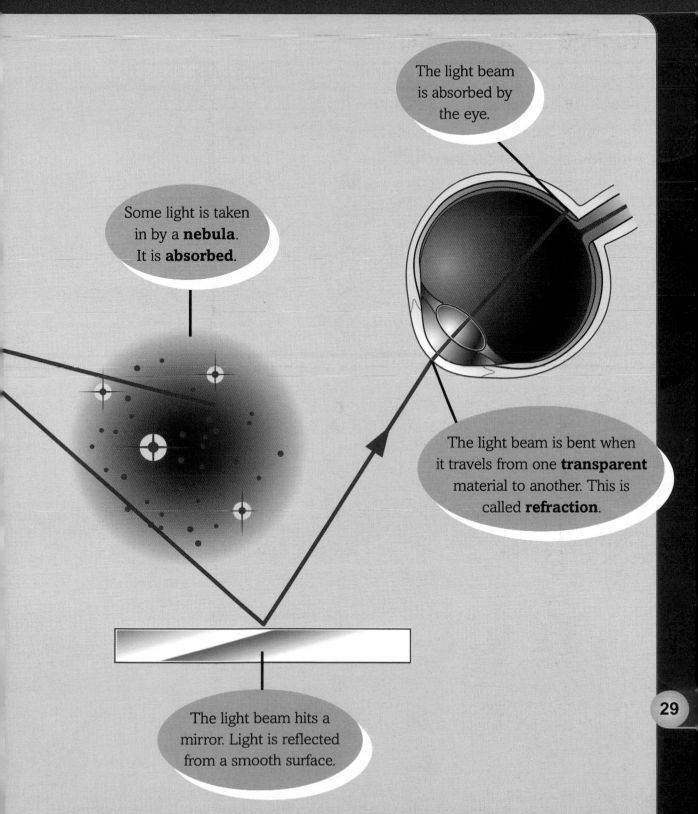

Glossary

absorbed taken in. A light beam is absorbed if it doesn't bounce off something.

atmosphere layer of air around Earth. Beyond the atmosphere is space.

constellation group of stars that make a pattern in the sky. Deneb is in the Swan constellation.

energy ability to make things move or change. A light beam is a type of energy.

focus bring light beams together to make a clear picture. A telescope can focus light beams.

galaxy enormous group of stars. Earth is in the Milky Way galaxy.

lens curved piece of glass or other material. A lens brings light beams together to make a clear picture.

light year distance light travels in a year. This is roughly 9500 billion kilometres (5900 billion miles).

nebula enormous cloud of gas and dust. Nebulas are found in space.

nerves thin threads inside the body that carry messages. Nerves run to and from your brain.

opaque something that stops light passing through it. Anything that casts a shadow is opaque.

reflected bounced off. A light beam can be reflected by a mirror for example.

refraction way that light bends when it moves from one transparent material to another. Light beams are refracted when they pass from space into the Earth's atmosphere.

retina coating on the back of the eye that picks up light. A nerve then sends the picture to your brain.

shadow patch of darkness made when an object is blocking out light. Your body makes a shadow when the sun shines when you're outside.

star huge burning ball of gas. The Sun is a star.

transparent something that lets light pass through it. Glass is transparent.

Want to know more?

Books

- *Discover Science: Light*, Kim Taylor (Chrysalis, 2005)
- *Horrible Science: Frightening Light*, Nick Arnold (Scholastic Hippo, 1999)
- *Light and Sight*, Jon Richards (Franklin Watts, 2002)
- *Inventor's Handbook: Light and Vision*, Keith Greaves and Andrea Aird (Silver Dolphin, 2002)
- *The Time and Space of Uncle Albert*, Russell Stannard (Faber and Faber, 1989)

Websites

- www.childrensmuseum.org/ cosmicquest/spacestation/index2.html To follow a light beam, you have to be able to live in space. Try this Cosmic Quest game to see if you could survive.
- www.amnh.org/exhibitions/ einstein/light/index.php Learn more about Albert Einstein and light at the American Museum of Natural History.

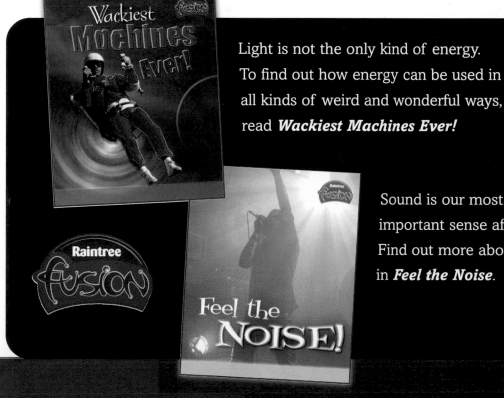

Light is not the only kind of energy. To find out how energy can be used in all kinds of weird and wonderful ways, read **Wackiest Machines Ever!**

Sound is our most important sense after sight. Find out more about sound in **Feel the Noise**.

Index